GONE FISHING
2025 CALENDAR

JANUARY 2025

SUNDAY	MONDAY	TUESDAY	WEDNESDAY	THURSDAY	FRIDAY	SATURDAY
29	30	31	1	2	3	4
5	6	7	8	9	10	11
12	13	14	15	16	17	18
19	20	21	22	23	24	25
26	27	28	29	30	31	1

FEBRUARY 2025

SUNDAY	MONDAY	TUESDAY	WEDNESDAY	THURSDAY	FRIDAY	SATURDAY
26	27	28	29	30	31	1
2	3	4	5	6	7	8
9	10	11	12	13	14	15
16	17	18	19	20	21	22
23	24	25	26	27	28	1

MARCH 2025

SUNDAY	MONDAY	TUESDAY	WEDNESDAY	THURSDAY	FRIDAY	SATURDAY
23	24	25	26	27	28	1
2	3	4	5	6	7	8
9	10	11	12	13	14	15
16	17	18	19	20	21	22
23	24	25	26	27	28	29
30	31					

APRIL 2025

SUNDAY	MONDAY	TUESDAY	WEDNESDAY	THURSDAY	FRIDAY	SATURDAY
30	31	1	2	3	4	5
6	7	8	9	10	11	12
13	14	15	16	17	18	19
20	21	22	23	24	25	26
27	28	29	30	1	2	3

MAY 2025

SUNDAY	MONDAY	TUESDAY	WEDNESDAY	THURSDAY	FRIDAY	SATURDAY
27	28	29	30	1	2	3
4	5	6	7	8	9	10
11	12	13	14	15	16	17
18	19	20	21	22	23	24
25	26	27	28	29	30	31

JUNE 2025

SUNDAY	MONDAY	TUESDAY	WEDNESDAY	THURSDAY	FRIDAY	SATURDAY
1	2	3	4	5	6	7
8	9	10	11	12	13	14
15	16	17	18	19	20	21
22	23	24	25	26	27	28
29	30	1	2	3	4	5

JULY 2025

SUNDAY	MONDAY	TUESDAY	WEDNESDAY	THURSDAY	FRIDAY	SATURDAY
29	30	1	2	3	4	5
6	7	8	9	10	11	12
13	14	15	16	17	18	19
20	21	22	23	24	25	26
27	28	29	30	31	1	2

AUGUST 2025

SUNDAY	MONDAY	TUESDAY	WEDNESDAY	THURSDAY	FRIDAY	SATURDAY
27	28	29	30	31	1	2
3	4	5	6	7	8	9
10	11	12	13	14	15	16
17	18	19	20	21	22	23
24 / 31	25	26	27	28	29	30

SEPTEMBER 2025

SUNDAY	MONDAY	TUESDAY	WEDNESDAY	THURSDAY	FRIDAY	SATURDAY
31	1	2	3	4	5	6
7	8	9	10	11	12	13
14	15	16	17	18	19	20
21	22	23	24	25	26	27
28	29	30	1	2	3	4

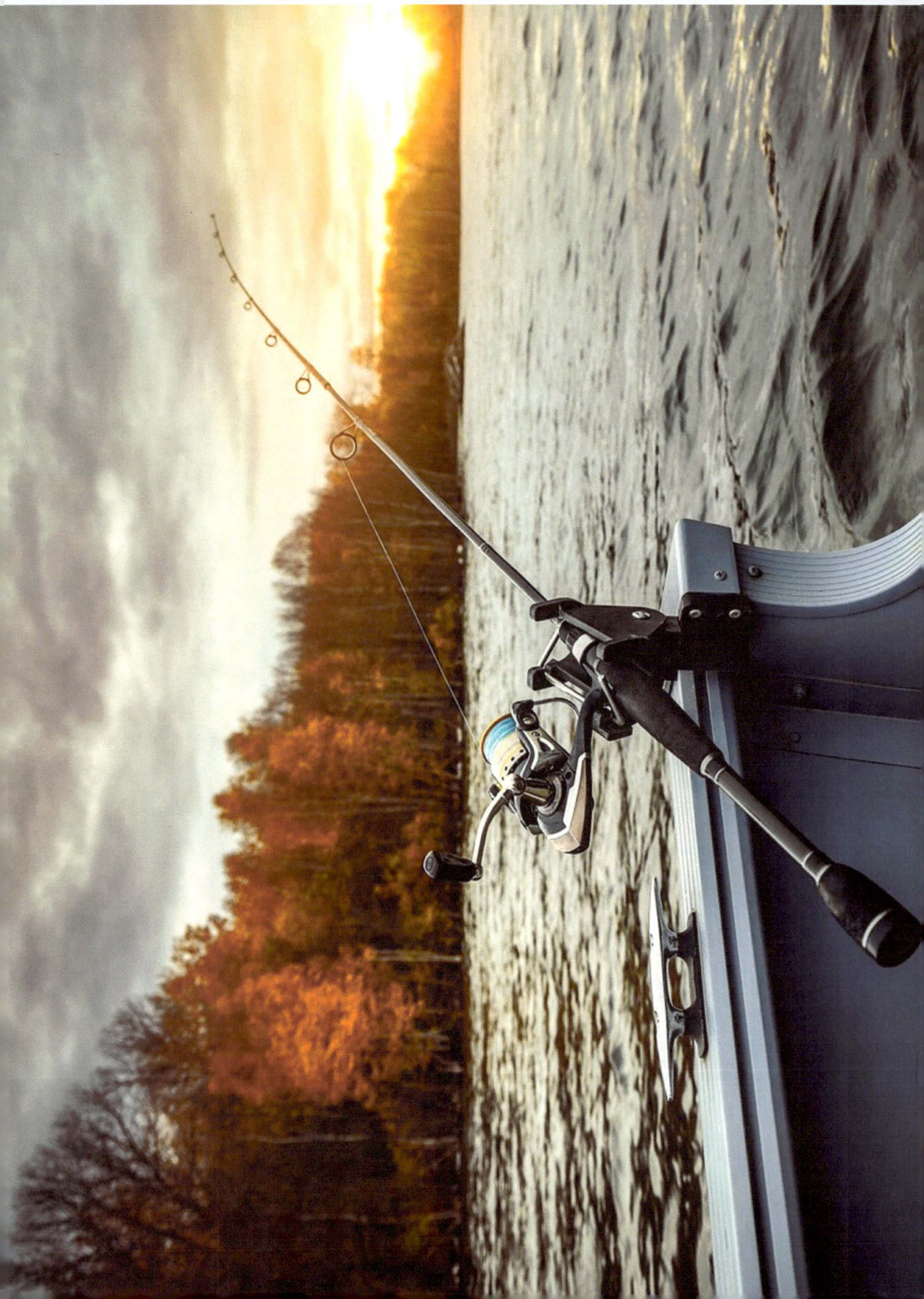

OCTOBER 2025

SUNDAY	MONDAY	TUESDAY	WEDNESDAY	THURSDAY	FRIDAY	SATURDAY
28	29	30	1	2	3	4
5	6	7	8	9	10	11
12	13	14	15	16	17	18
19	20	21	22	23	24	25
26	27	28	29	30	31	1

NOVEMBER 2025

SUNDAY	MONDAY	TUESDAY	WEDNESDAY	THURSDAY	FRIDAY	SATURDAY
26	27	28	29	30	31	1
2	3	4	5	6	7	8
9	10	11	12	13	14	15
16	17	18	19	20	21	22
23	24	25	26	27	28	29
30						

DECEMBER 2025

SUNDAY	MONDAY	TUESDAY	WEDNESDAY	THURSDAY	FRIDAY	SATURDAY
30	1	2	3	4	5	6
7	8	9	10	11	12	13
14	15	16	17	18	19	20
21	22	23	24	25	26	27
28	29	30	31	1	2	3

30 OF THE BEST FISHING SPOTS IN THE WORLD

Lake Baikal, Russia: Known for its unique biodiversity and record-breaking depths.

Lake Victoria, Africa: The largest lake in Africa, teeming with Nile perch and tilapia.

Amazon River Basin, South America: Home to diverse species like peacock bass and piranha.

Lake Tanganyika, Africa: Holds some of the world's most unique fish species.

Mekong River, Southeast Asia: Famous for giant catfish and other large freshwater species.

Lake Malawi, Africa: Renowned for its colorful cichlid fish species.

Great Lakes, USA/Canada: Includes Lakes Superior, Michigan, Huron, Erie, and Ontario, rich with various fish species.

Fraser River, Canada: Known for its abundant salmon and sturgeon populations.

Lake Nasser, Egypt: Famous for Nile perch fishing.

Fly-fishing in New Zealand: Especially in the rivers and lakes of the South Island.

Volga River, Russia: Renowned for its large catfish and pike.

Lake Kariba, Zambia/Zimbabwe: Known for tigerfish and tilapia.

Colorado River, USA: Noted for its rainbow trout and bass fishing.

Amazon Rainforest, Brazil: Diverse species like peacock bass, arowana, and piranha.

Lake of the Woods, USA/Canada: Offers excellent walleye, bass, and muskie fishing.

Taimen Fishing in Mongolia: Home to the giant taimen, a species of trout.

Inle Lake, Myanmar: Known for its traditional fishing methods and rich biodiversity.

Yukon River, Canada/USA: Abundant in salmon, grayling, and northern pike.

Loch Ness, Scotland: Beyond the legend of Nessie, it offers great trout fishing.

Lake Okeechobee, USA: Famous for largemouth bass fishing.

Zambezi River, Africa: Renowned for its aggressive tigerfish.

Okavango Delta, Botswana: A unique ecosystem with diverse fish species.

Kenai River, Alaska, USA: Known for its king salmon and rainbow trout.

Lake Geneva, Switzerland/France: Offers excellent perch and trout fishing.

Bristol Bay, Alaska, USA: Premier spot for salmon fishing.

St. Lawrence River, USA/Canada: Renowned for its muskie and bass fishing.

Lake Tana, Ethiopia: Rich in diverse fish species, including large Nile perch.

Lake Winnipeg, Canada: Known for its huge walleye.

Patagonia, Argentina/Chile: World-class fly-fishing destination for trout.

Lake Bled, Slovenia: Picturesque setting with abundant carp and trout fishing.

30 OF THE MOST POPULAR FRESH WATER FISH

Largemouth Bass: A top sport fish in North America, known for its size and fight.

Smallmouth Bass: Popular for its fighting ability and preference for clearer, rocky waters.

Rainbow Trout: Valued for its beautiful coloration and presence in cold-water streams and lakes.

Brown Trout: Sought after for its elusive nature and challenging catch.

Brook Trout: A favorite among fly fishermen for its vibrant colors and presence in cool, clean waters.

Walleye: Prized for its tasty fillets and popularity in northern U.S. and Canadian waters.

Northern Pike: Known for its aggressive nature and large size.

Muskellunge (Muskie): The "fish of 10,000 casts" due to its elusive nature and trophy size.

Bluegill: A common panfish, popular for beginners and kids.

Crappie (Black and White): Highly sought after for its tasty meat and school-forming behavior.

Channel Catfish: A favorite for its size and presence in warm waters.

Flathead Catfish: Known for its large size and predatory behavior.

Common Carp: Popular in Europe and Asia for sport fishing.

Koi: Ornamental variety of carp, popular in ponds and aquariums.

Tilapia: Widely farmed and known for its mild-flavored meat.

Peacock Bass: Valued for its aggressive nature and vibrant colors, especially in South America.

Nile Perch: Popular in African waters for its size and fight.

Taimen: Known as the "river wolf," a large and aggressive fish in Mongolia.

Arctic Char: Similar to trout, found in cold Arctic and sub-Arctic waters.

Sockeye Salmon: Prized for its red flesh and challenging migration runs.

Chinook (King) Salmon: The largest of the Pacific salmon, valued for sport and eating.

Coho Salmon: Known for its fight and quality meat.

Lake Trout: A large predator found in deep, cold lakes.

Sturgeon: Ancient fish known for its size and caviar.

Grayling: Recognizable by its sail-like dorsal fin, popular among fly anglers.

Pikeperch (Zander): European cousin to the walleye, prized for its meat.

Perch (Yellow and European): Common panfish known for its sweet, flaky meat.

Oscar: Popular aquarium fish known for its intelligence and personality.

Arapaima: Large South American fish known for its size and air-breathing ability.

Gourami (Various species): Popular in aquariums for their unique appearance and behavior.

www.ingramcontent.com/pod-product-compliance
Lightning Source LLC
Chambersburg PA
CBHW041105050426
42335CB00046B/137